BEFORE WE EAT

from farm to table

Pat Brisson   Illustrated by Mary Azarian

TILBURY HOUSE PUBLISHERS, THOMASTON, MAINE

As we sit around this table
let's give thanks as we are able

to all the folks we'll never meet
who helped provide this food we eat.

They plowed the ground

and planted seeds,

tended fields,

removed the weeds.

They picked the food at harvest time,

working in the heat and grime.

They grazed the cattle,

fed the sows,

gathered eggs,

and milked the cows.

They fished from boats

out on the seas;

raised wheat

and nuts and honeybees.

Thank the ones who packed the crates,

sorted boxes, checked the weights.

Thank the drivers on the roads

in their trucks with heavy loads.

And all the clerks at all the stores

who did the grocery-selling chores.

Thank the ones who bought this food,

the ones who teach me gratitude.

Sitting at this meal we share,
we are grateful and aware,

sending thanks upon the air . . .

to those workers everywhere.

Plant a Garden with Your Kids

from the Appalachian Sustainable Agriculture Project

Children are naturally curious. Let them outdoors, give them a chance to see nature at work, and their curiosity about natural systems will know no bounds.

That's what makes edible gardens such a great learning tool. Engaging children in gardening gets them outdoors and inspires awe and wonder. Planting an edible (yes, edible—so much more to interact with!) garden helps children figure out where their food comes from, how plants grow from seed to vegetable or fruit, what grows when, and how delicious a fresh tomato tastes. Children can see firsthand that kohlrabi

looks bizarre enough to have been grown on Mars and that green beans can be purple, carrots can be red, and potatoes can be blue. Children who have grown fresh vegetables eat them with gusto, and a garden cultivates a child's innate sense of curiosity while it grows delicious, healthy food.

If you don't know how to garden, enlist a

volunteer gardener to help—a friend, neighbor, or local farmer. Information abounds in books and websites, and you will be modeling the learning process as you go. The barriers are minimal: You need dirt, nutrients, seeds, and water. You don't need grant money; would you write a grant before planting a garden in your backyard? You don't need a field; a raised bed in an asphalt schoolyard will suffice.

If you want to connect what you're doing in the garden to classroom instruction, ASAP's Growing Minds Farm to School program has extensive resources—including a searchable database of children's literature, lesson plans, videos on cafeteria taste tests and classroom cooking, and more—at www.growing-minds. org. Connect nationally with the National Farm to School Network at www.farmtoschool.org.

Ready, set, plant!

Local Food
Strong Farms
Healthy Communities

Make a Seed Tape

To Plant in Your Own Garden

from the Appalachian Sustainable Agriculture Project

WHAT YOU WILL NEED:

biodegradable paper strips, cornstarch paste, seeds, ruler, pencil, Q-tips or paintbrush, tweezers or fingers

1

Choose your seed!

2

Use your pencil and ruler to mark correct spacing for each seed type. See your seed packet or container for specific spacing.

3

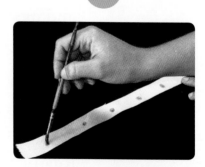

Use a paintbrush or Q-tip to spread small dots of cornstarch paste on each of your pencil marks.

4

Place 1 or 2 seeds on each dot of paste using fingers or tweezers.

5

If needed, cover your seeds with a little more cornstarch paste to make sure the seeds stick!

6

Allow your seed tape to dry, place it in a paper bag, and it is ready to take home and plant. Simply lay the tape in the soil, seed-side up, at the depth recommended on the seed packet.

Further Resources

http://njaes.rutgers.edu/pubs/fs1211/

A school garden provides a pathway for learning about science and nature, math, reading, music, art, and teamwork. The website of the New Jersey Agricultural Experiment Station at Rutgers University and its associated Cooperative Extension Service shows how. There are Cooperative Extension services at land-grant universities across America, and a few minutes of browsing will take you to one near you!

www.edutopia.org/blog/garden-based-learning-kristin-stayer

Supported by the George Lucas Education Foundation, this blog is a good compilation of information and community resources for garden-based learning.

www.greeneducationfoundation.org/greenthumbchallengesub/curriculum-and-activities/ garden-activity-center/713-science-in-the-garden.html

From the website: "Gardens provide opportunities for kids to explore and learn about the natural world—at a time when they are increasingly separated from it. Invite your students to be soil detectives, plant observers and insect identifyers! Plant gardens that welcome wildlife and enhance the biodiversity of your space."

www.farmtoschool.org

The National Farm to School Network is an information, advocacy, and networking hub for communities working to bring local food sourcing, school gardens, and food and agriculture education into schools and early care and education settings across the country. Their website offers resources for getting started with farm-to-school programs and school gardens; research on the benefits of farm-to-school activities; and connections with farm-to-school and local food experts in communities across America.

www.growing-minds.org

Growing Minds works with schools in 60 Appalachian counties to provide farm-to-school experiences for students. This is one of the first farm-to-school programs in the country, with a resource-rich website full of lesson plans, recipes, a searchable database of children's literature on local food and farming, advice on school gardens, and much more.

Manley, Reeser, and Marjorie Peronto, *The Life in Your Garden: Gardening for Biodiversity*. Tilbury House Publishers, 2016. This is a book for adults, but its message about gardening for the health of the planet will resonate with kids.

For my grandchildren: Baxley, Madeline, Azalea, Pender, Eamon, Abigail, and Mia —PB

With utmost respect for small farmers everywhere on Earth—stewards
of the land, heart of community —MA

TILBURY HOUSE PUBLISHERS
12 Starr Street, Thomaston, Maine 04861
800-582-1899 • www.tilburyhouse.com

Hardcover ISBN 978-088448-652-7

First hardcover printing of the first edition: May 2014
First hardcover printing of the second edition: March 2018

15 16 17 18 19 20 XXX 10 9 8 7 6 5 4

Designed by Geraldine Millham, Westport, Massachusetts
Backmatter design by Frame25 Productions
Printed and bound in South Korea

PAT BRISSON (at left in this photo) has written 20 books for young readers, including *The Summer My Father Was Ten* and *Sometimes We Were Brave*. She is a former school teacher, school librarian, and public library reference librarian.

MARY AZARIAN (right) lives and works on a hilltop farm in Vermont and is the Caldecott Medal–winning illustrator of *Snowflake Bentley*. She created the illustrations for *Before We Eat* by first carving the pictures in wood (in reverse!) and then printing them with ink onto paper before adding color with acrylic paints.